COLLABORATION THROUGH CONSULTATION

A Powerful Tool for Building Community

by Sara DeHoff

Collaboration through Consultation: A Powerful Tool for Community Building

Sara DeHoff

ISBN: 978-1-951000-00-4

Published by Our Prosperous World
www.OurProsperousWorld.com

Requests to publish work from this book should be sent to:
sarad@ourprosperousworld.com

Cover design and illustration: Carlos Brito
Interior design: Laura Boyle

*For Dad, who is my guiding light
and the inspiration for my work.*

*For Uncle John, who sits on my other shoulder
and keeps me going.*

CONTENTS

PREFACE

In my 30 years of working with groups of all kinds, one of the most powerful tools I have found for collective action and group learning is consultation. It's a process of truth-seeking that is built on consensus and strives to find the best possible solution for all concerned.

Much like the "talking stick" from the Native American tradition and the idea of mindfulness from Buddhism, the concept of consultation is the Bahá'í community's contribution to humanity's collective wisdom about working together. The principles outlined here are based on the framework provided by Bahá'u'lláh and further explained by 'Abdu'l-Bahá and Shoghi Effendi. Since the Bahá'í community has no clergy, consultation is the essential means for decision-making by its elected governing bodies. Because this process is so effective in gathering wisdom and getting everyone on board, it is used in all Bahá'í community endeavors, formal and informal, large and small.

Just as you don't need to be a tribal member to use a talking stick or become a Buddhist to benefit from mindfulness, you don't need to be a Bahá'í to use consultation. These principles are universal and can work in any setting.

I wrote this book for change makers, collaborators, coaches, and all those who see the possibility of a better world and are working to achieve it. Such a world is possible when we pool our talents and work together. Consultation is a powerful tool for making this happen. It can be used by:

- Executive teams charting the course of their nonprofits.
- Social entrepreneurs working with their constituents to find the best way to address a need.
- Coaches offering tools for work teams and families.
- Human resources professionals helping employees work effectively in teams.
- Community organizations seeking a way to address local concerns.
- And many more…

Since consultation is a tool for learning as well as for collective action, I'd love to hear what you learn as you apply these principles. The more we learn from each other, the faster we can progress in building a just, peaceful, dynamic human civilization.

Sara DeHoff
ourprosperousworld.com

Introduction
THE BUTTERFLY STORY

For some time now, scientists have been studying the butterfly and how it transforms from a lowly caterpillar to a winged beauty. This is what they've found…

The caterpillar goes through most of its life in a mild-mannered way, crawling and munching. At a certain point, it develops a voracious appetite and consumes everything in sight, growing larger and larger. Finally, it finds a nice spot, hangs from a leaf and forms a chrysalis around itself.

Inside the caterpillar are specialized cells, known as seminal cells or "imaginal" cells, that know how to make a butterfly. However, the caterpillar's immune system sees these cells as foreign bodies and destroys them. That is, until enough of the imaginal cells emerge, *find each other* and start working together. Then the caterpillar becomes the nutritional soup out of which the butterfly is made.

It's an interesting parallel to what's happening in the world today. Our voracious rate of consumption is wreaking havoc on the very systems that sustain us. Yet, at the same time, individuals and groups are coming together to solve problems and build new systems at the local, regional and international levels. These are our own version of imaginal cells.

So this book is for you: the change makers, collaborators and coaches, the activists and advisors. It's for everyone who dreams of a better world. We *are* the imaginal cells. We *know* things can be better and we choose to *act* to make it happen. As we learn how to come together and work together, we will see this world transform from the inside out.

Consultation is a powerful tool for building this vision. It's a way to learn together, combine our talents and amplify our efforts, opening up new ways of collaborating.

So for all of you who dare to build the butterfly, this book is for you.

Never doubt that a small group of thoughtful,
committed citizens can change the world;
indeed, it's the only thing that ever has.

~ Margaret Mead

Chapter 1
CONSULTATION

We live in a world that is fractured, contentious and rapidly catapulting toward social and environmental upheaval. We humans face staggering problems on a global scale and yet we've become entangled in polarized arguments about what the problems are and what to do about them. We've become immobilized. Even at the local level, the problems are complex and intertwined. How can we improve school performance without also addressing poverty, racism, unemployment and equity?

Individuals working alone cannot do much to solve these challenges. It is by working together and learning as we go that we'll actually find solutions that work for everyone. Now, more than ever, we humans are being called upon to collaborate in groups of greater and greater diversity. We are having to learn by doing, as our old answers no longer work. We need to learn together so we can tap into the immense creativity of the human spirit and find solutions to the interconnected issues we face. None of us can do it alone.

However, the problem with groups is they can easily devolve into wrangling factions, personal agendas (whether hidden or not) and dominance by the powerful (or loudest). No doubt you've experienced group dysfunction of one type or another. But what if it didn't have to be this way? What if there was a way for groups to really work well and create great things together?

Consultation is a process of group decision-making that seeks out the truth of an issue and strives to find the best possible solution. It provides a means for groups to fully understand the matter at hand, come to a consensus about it and arrive at a collective course of action. It's a valuable tool that can be used in any group, including:

- Executive teams
- Work teams
- Boards of directors
- Managerial groups
- Business organizations
- Families
- International institutions
- Governing bodies
- Community organizations
- Schools
- Neighborhoods

Say: no man can attain his true station except through his justice. No power can exist except through unity. No welfare and well-being can be attained except through consultation.

~ Bahá'u'lláh

HOW DOES CONSULTATION WORK?

Consultation involves both principles and process. We'll explore each of these further in the following chapters.

Principles

- **Oneness of humanity:** We humans are one species, one race, one human family. We are infinitely varied in how we express ourselves through language, culture, dress and customs, but we are one people. Once we understand this, everything else flows from here.

- **Harmony and Inspiration:** Simply put, a team that respects and appreciates one another is going to be far more effective than one that bickers. A team whose members reach beyond themselves and are inspired by a higher vision will tap into creativity they didn't know they had.

- **Inner Work:** Group work is only half the equation. The other half is the inner work each of us must do individually to develop spiritual qualities such as patience, service, humility, etc.

Process

1. **Express your view:** When grappling with an issue, each participant must be free to fully express his or her view. The flip side is that you must also listen carefully to the views of the other participants. You never know who will come up with the next gem of wisdom.

2. **Let it go:** Once you've stated your view, let go of it completely. Now the view belongs to the group.

3. **Seek truth:** The group then explores all the different views—sorting, sifting, combining, evaluating—to arrive at the truth of the matter.

4. **Support the decision:** Once the group makes a decision, everyone supports it, whether they agree or not. If the decision is wrong, it will quickly become apparent and a new decision can be made.

While these concepts of consultation are easy to understand, implementing them takes practice. When I feel strongly about something, it's difficult to let go of my opinion on the matter. It's hard not to react when someone voices an opposing view. But all of this is necessary if the group is going to consult effectively.

VACATION PLANS

Here's how consultation helped my family...

Last spring, we were planning our family vacation. This is always a tricky thing for me. Our teenage daughter wants something active and adventurous. My husband's work is quite intense and he just needs a rest. I feel like I'm caught in the middle trying to broker a deal between the two of them. Usually we end up with a compromise that no one really wants.

As I began working on this consultation material, I suddenly realized, "We're not consulting!" So I went back to them and suggested we try this approach. We sat down and discussed our vacation again. This time, each of us was very frank and open about what we wanted and needed. And then we let it go.

As a result, we were able to come up with a plan that suited everyone—a great balance of adventure, new sights, vigorous activity and peaceful strolls, all in a beautiful setting. It was the best vacation we've ever had. Several times a day, one or more of us would just burst out with "This is so much fun!"

And it wasn't just because we consulted in the beginning; we carried that consultative attitude with us throughout the trip. When something came up or things didn't go according to plan, we regrouped, discussed it some more and came up with a solution that everyone was happy with. More than anything, it was this spirit of willingness that made everything so special. We each knew we would be heard and we discovered that by combining our ideas we usually came up with much better solutions. It really was a great trip. And we've been able to carry over what we learned there to our day-to-day lives. Talk about well-being!

PUTTING IT INTO PRACTICE

So how do we start? We'll cover the various aspects of consultation in the following chapters. For now, just observe:

- **Listen.**
  Listen carefully to the conversations in your group, work team or family. What kinds of conversations do you have?

- **Notice.**
  What do you notice about these conversations? What words would you use to describe them?

WHAT DOES THIS MAKE POSSIBLE?

Can you imagine if our governments, our businesses, our schools all worked on the principle of seeking truth in every matter? Or if we started every endeavor from the principle of oneness—seeing every human being as a valuable member of the human family? Just think what we could accomplish!

WHAT IS YOUR EXPERIENCE?

- When have you experienced a group that worked well together?
- What happened?
- How did it happen?
- What made it successful?

Assemble, speak together: let your minds be all
of one accord... United be the thoughts of all
that all may happily agree.

~ Vedas, Rig Veda - Book 10

Chapter 2
ONENESS OF HUMANITY

We humans have become accustomed to seeing ourselves in conflict with one another. We argue about values, we polarize around issues. Every day the news brings fresh stories of us versus them. This culture of contest permeates every aspect of our lives, from business and sports, to politics and the justice system. This is what we see around us and it shapes our thinking.

But our reality is that we humans are one people, one global family. Like the cells of the body, we constitute one organic whole. Each cell contributes to the health of the body and derives its nourishment from it. No cell exists outside the body and the body fully functions only when all its cells are working harmoniously together.

So it is with humankind. Each of us has a contribution to make and each of us benefits from being part of the whole.

This is the oneness of humanity. It's not about uniformity—that somehow I must make everyone think the way I think. This oneness, this unity, *embraces* diversity. In fact, it requires it. The body needs all the different types of cells that make up its bones, brain, muscles and organs. If all the cells were the same, the body could not function.

The implications of this principle are immense. It affects all aspects of human life, from personal interactions to international relations. The oneness of humanity calls for:

- Treating every human being with dignity and respect.
- Abandoning prejudices of all kinds: class, creed, race, sex, color, nation, economic status, etc.
- Seeing all people as one human family.
- Balancing current economic needs with the environmental needs of future generations.
- Seeing the world as one country, the home of humankind.

The principle of the Oneness of Mankind... implies an organic change in the structure of present-day society, a change such as the world has not yet experienced.

[It] calls for no less than the reconstruction and the demilitarization of the whole civilized world—a world organically unified in all the essential aspects of its life,

its political machinery,
its spiritual aspiration,
its trade and finance,
its script and language,

and yet infinite in the diversity of the national
characteristics of its federated units.

~ Shoghi Effendi

This is a vast vision. And it begins with coming together, working together, practicing these skills of consultation and learning from our experience.

In consultation, our diversity allows us to see an issue from many perspectives. Our unity allows us to gather the wisdom from those perspectives and chart a wise course of action.

PUTTING DIFFERENCES TO WORK

Some time ago, I took a class on color and the impact it has on our lives. I was intrigued by how each color can have different meanings and how those meanings change from culture to culture. Orange indicates abundance, but it can also mean caution. Black is sophisticated and yet can be heavy and oppressive. The color for royalty in the West is purple, but in China, the emperor's color is yellow. There are so many layers and varieties of meanings.

Not long afterward, I was outside when the sun broke through the clouds and a rainbow appeared. As I gazed at the shimmering colors, I realized that these billions of raindrops are all individually refracting the sunlight—every single raindrop contains the entire rainbow within it.

We are like these raindrops. Each one of us contains all of these qualities: intelligence, precision, nobility, happiness, growth, renewal, peace, energy and abundance. It's just that we each possess these qualities in different proportions. Some of us are really good at analytical thinking. Some of us are really good at connecting with people. Some of us focus on seeking deeper spiritual meanings.

It's easy to get frustrated with people who think differently from ourselves. But the truth is, we all have all these qualities, even if some are in tiny amounts. And when we learn to value these qualities in each other, we start to see how they complement one another. Together we form a complete rainbow.

Let me give you an example.

My sister, Meg, loves math. She's a whiz with numbers. Excel spreadsheets are among her favorite tools. And she loves order. She finds immense satisfaction in finding a place for everything. Not only does she find the right box for something, she makes it look pretty too.

I'm not this way. My world is the world of words and ideas. I'm fascinated with stories. I don't like to take the time to put things away because… "Oh! I just had an idea! Quick, where's a pen? I've got to capture it before it disappears!" And then I end up with piles of paper scraps everywhere (along with the piles of all the things I haven't yet put away).

You can imagine there was a bit of tension between us growing up, sharing a bedroom. Meg threatened to paint a line down the center of the room in an attempt to contain my mess to my half. And I got frustrated with everything having to be exactly in its place.

Believe it or not, we actually went into business together as adults. And we quickly learned to put our diversity to work. Meg, as the numbers person, managed the finances and the inventory (we imported rayon batik fabrics from

Bali). Our little warehouse was the neatest, most organized place you could imagine. Every bolt of fabric had its place and was clearly labeled. Filling orders was so easy!

I worked on the designs and the marketing. It was so much fun to find the artists and create the images and color schemes. I was also in charge of creating the website and telling our story.

When we traveled to Bali to work with the factory, our diversity had an added bonus. Meg mastered the Indonesian money immediately, while I still fumbled with making change. However, I had an ear for languages. So when we got into the taxi, I gave the driver directions and Meg paid him once we arrived.

Both of us were relieved not to have to worry about the thing we weren't good at and focus on the things that came easily for us. Oh, we still tangled with one another occasionally—when we tried to make the other person more like ourselves. But we'd quickly snap out of it because it was our differences that were our strength.

We weren't polar opposites either; we each had some talent in both areas. I helped with the books and Meg helped with the designs. It's just that those weren't our strong points. In the process of working together, we came to really value the other person's strengths. It was very clear that, together, we formed a whole.

Epilogue: To finish the story... We successfully created and sold a line of rayon batik fabrics to fabric stores and designers here in the U.S. and Canada. We eventually discovered that, while those who love rayon batiks really love them, there weren't enough of them to keep the business going. So we ended up shutting it down.

The intensity of that time of working and learning together has brought us much closer together than either of us could have imagined. Neither of us would trade that experience for anything.

In all things that are purely social we can be as separate as the fingers, yet one as the hand in all things essential to mutual progress.

~ Booker T. Washington

PUTTING IT INTO PRACTICE

So how do we foster this oneness? Here's a place to begin:

1. **See everyone in your group as an essential part of the whole.**

   Each member of your team has something valuable to contribute, and it may be very different from what you bring to the table.

   When you feel yourself starting to get frustrated with certain individuals, pause for a moment. What is happening in the group? How is this person seeing the issue differently? Relax your mind and just listen to what the person has to say. What insights does he or she bring?

2. **Understand that everyone at the table is there to help your group succeed.**

   We are all champions of justice, compatriots in a global movement to make the world a better place.

   When we address each other with this attitude, we call forth our own nobility and that of everyone on the team. There's an old Norwegian proverb:

   "In every woman there is a Queen.
   Speak to the Queen and the Queen will answer."

   When we speak to the highest in each of us, our highest nature responds.

3. **Identify the strengths each person brings to the table.**
   Who can you count on to take a practical, pragmatic view? Who is looking off into the future? Who counts the pennies? Which of you cares deeply about the well-being of the people? Who is concerned about structure and organization? All of these are strengths and all of them are valuable. In fact, you'll need all these strengths to be successful. The challenge is seeing them all as part of the whole.

4. **Appreciate each other.**
   Acknowledge each other for what you bring to the table. The next time the pragmatic person speaks up, thank her—she helps keep your feet on the ground. When your visionary starts talking about what you can accomplish in the future, thank him—he helps you dream up new tomorrows. When your "people person" starts talking about how this will affect the people around you, thank her—she helps you stay connected to your community, the source of your resources. When your quiet person speaks up, thank him—very often he'll bring insights everyone else has missed. Honor each other for the unique strengths you each bring, because now your team has access to all of these qualities.

The lamps are different, but the
Light is the same.

~ Rumi

WHAT DOES THIS MAKE POSSIBLE?

Can you imagine what could happen if your group sees itself as a whole that is greater than the sum of its parts? What if your group saw itself as an essential part of a larger whole—the family of humanity? What impact does your work have on the world?

WHAT IS YOUR EXPERIENCE?

- When have you experienced different people coming together for a common purpose?
- Was it easy or difficult to find the unity in your diversity?
- What helped your group build unity or a shared vision?
- How did your group's diversity help your group function?

Chapter 3

HARMONY AND INSPIRATION

Have you ever experienced a group that just doesn't get along? Personalities grate on each other and differences become sticking points. Small problems grow and big problems become ordeals. Working together is like pulling teeth. No one looks forward to the meetings and the process becomes one of resigned endurance rather than dynamic creativity.

HARMONY

But look what happens when a group starts to appreciate one another's differences and value each other's contributions. Even small gestures can make a big difference, such as thanking someone for the effort they put in or appreciating a colleague for offering a fresh perspective.

When a group chooses appreciation and respect, it's like the clouds clear and the sun comes out. Everyone listens, everyone is heard and everyone is valued. When a group agrees to do their work in harmony rather than in contention, the differences between people become a source of strength. Like notes in a chord, their uniqueness harmonizes as each person brings their best to the table. Removing conflict releases creativity.

The more we see each other as fellow compatriots and champions of truth, the more effective our work becomes. We each come into the consultative process with both strengths and limitations. The more we focus on building unity, the easier it is to weave our strengths together and find solutions. What emerges is love—seeing the best in each other and encouraging it.

INSPIRATION

When we reach beyond ourselves, we are much more able to work together. However you conceive of this is entirely up to you. For those with a religious bent, you may describe it as turning to God, Allah, the Universe, the Tao, the Great Spirit or whatever you call the great Unknowable Essence. For others, this might look more like reaching for the best of who we really are—those universal qualities that make us truly human: compassion, truth, and justice.

Consultation requires each of us to look beyond our own wants and desires to that which is eternal, divine and universal within each of us. And it requires of us humility to realize that we don't have all the answers. Working together, though, we'll find them.

The first condition is absolute
love and harmony
amongst the members...
for they are the waves of one sea,
the drops of one river,
the stars of one heaven,
the rays of one sun,
the trees of one orchard,
the flowers of one garden.
The second condition: They must when coming
together turn their faces to the Kingdom on
High and ask aid
from the Realm of Glory.

~ 'Abdu'l-Baha

COMMUNITY THEATER

Years ago, I got involved in the Fleetwood-Jourdain Theater, an African-American community theater in Evanston, just north of Chicago. I just showed up one day to volunteer and they graciously allowed me to stay. Most of the time, I was the only white person in the building.

Rehearsals were underway for Sophisticated Lady, a musical of Duke Ellington's songs. Saturday afternoon came and we were scheduled to do our first "run-through", which is to go through the show from start to finish without stopping. Up to this time, people had been rehearsing parts of the show in small groups. This was the first time everyone came together—cast, crew, the band, everyone.

There were a lot of preparations to be made and details to work out. Finally everything was ready and we did the run-through. Oh man, was it rough! Mistakes, dropped lines, missed cues, you name it. We were like a rag-tag bunch of individuals all clamoring in the same space.

Gwethalyn Bronner, the director, gathered us all backstage for an Umoja Circle. I will never forget what happened next.

All of us—cast, crew and band—formed a circle and joined hands. Someone started chanting "Umoja means unity" (Umoja is a Swahili word) and everyone joined in.

We chanted for quite some time and gradually we could feel ourselves become more in sync with each other. We started to relax and just be part of the music we were creating together.

After a while the chant quieted and we hummed the melody as Gweth started talking. She shared with us her vision for this musical, what it meant to her and what it would mean to the audience. She talked about how each and every one of us was an essential part of the show. She talked about what she saw in us and what we could do together. Then, as we continued to hum softly, we went around the circle and each person shared what was in their heart—hopes and fears, love and appreciation, joy and humor, gratitude and prayers. Tears come to my eyes every time I recount this story.

When we'd all finished sharing, Gweth began again and, with stirring words, inspired us with her vision for this show. The chant started up again, building and building until it ended in a huge shout of triumph. I turned to the guy next to me, a member of the band whom I'd never met before, and suddenly realized he was my brother. We all embraced joyfully and set off to run through the show again. By this time it was 9 pm and we'd already put in a full day. But we were energized and ready to go. We did another run-through and this time it was a show!

The day will come when, after harnessing space, the winds, the tides and gravitation, we shall harness for God the energies of love. And on that day, for the second time in the history of the world, we shall have discovered fire.

~ Pierre Tielhard de Chardin

PUTTING IT INTO PRACTICE

So how do we create an atmosphere of harmony and inspiration in a group?

1. **Be willing.**
    The Fleetwood-Jourdain Community Theater had developed this Umoja Circle technique over time. Many of the people there had experienced it before and knew how powerful it was. Some of us were new and participated in it for the first time. What struck me was the willingness and the openness in that group: everyone arrived in the circle willing to not just participate, but to *contribute* to building a spirit of unity.

2. **Look for opportunities to appreciate people.**
    Especially when things have been tense in a group, it can take some practice to develop a pattern of appreciating one another. But look for small opportunities. The wonderful thing about working in a group is that you don't have to be good at everything. Do what you do well and really appreciate those whose skills complement your own. No one person has to do it all. What a relief!

3. **Focus on a common purpose.**
    Years ago a friend provided a wonderful description of marriage: If both spouses just focus on each other and move toward each other, it's like a line between two points; it's unstable and eventually collapses. But if both spouses focus on God and move toward God, they

form a triangle, which is stable. As both spouses move closer to God, they also move closer to each other.

The same is true for a group—if we focus on a common purpose, we all draw closer together as we move closer to our goal. Our differences become strengths, rather than points of contention. We start to see how to put our own unique talents to work for that purpose and we also start to see the gifts that every other member of the group brings to the table.

WHAT DOES THIS MAKE POSSIBLE?

Yes, a group can function on a purely intellectual level, but once you have a taste of what you can accomplish together with harmony and respect, you never want to go back. There's so much you can accomplish together! And it has a ripple effect well beyond the group itself. At the community theater, you should've seen the joy in the audience when they saw the performance. It was magic!

WHAT IS YOUR EXPERIENCE?

- When have you experienced a group that has attained a high level of harmony and respect?
- What helps create such an atmosphere?
- What is your experience with groups that reach beyond themselves for inspiration, aid and guidance?

Behold, how good and how pleasant it is for
brethren to dwell together in unity!

~ Psalms 133:1

Chapter 4
INNER WORK

Consultation takes practice and a focus on developing qualities within ourselves. If we come into it thinking that our ideas are the best ones and that everyone else should listen to us, we won't get very far as a group. But if we come into the group with patience, humility and a desire to serve a higher purpose, some amazing things can happen.

The prime requisites for them that take counsel together are purity of motive, radiance of spirit, detachment from all else save God, attraction to His Divine Fragrances, humility and lowliness amongst His loved ones, patience and long-suffering in difficulties and servitude to His exalted Threshold. Should they be graciously aided to acquire these attributes, victory from the unseen Kingdom of Bahá shall be vouchsafed to them.

~ 'Abdu'l-Bahá

Purity of motive, radiance of spirit, detachment... This is a tall order. Sometimes I'm not quite sure how to get my head around it all. What does radiance of spirit look like? How do I fully engage and yet be detached at the same time?

I've had the good fortune of meeting some extraordinary people who embody these qualities. When I need an example of what this looks like, these are the stories that come to mind...

CIRCLE TIME

Mrs. Weeratunga is a gifted teacher who has truly found her calling. She owns a Montessori school and was my daughter's preschool teacher. Talk about radiance of spirit! She just has this gentle glow about her all the time. She is the most patient person I've ever met. She doesn't put up with nonsense, but if you are striving toward something, she has all the time in the world for you.

She sees each of her little ones—more than 50 children between the ages of three and five—as a unique human being and treats them with dignity and respect. She understands their need and drive for mastery and serves that need with every fiber of her being. And the children love her.

When we went to visit the school to see if it was a good place for our daughter, we got there just as Circle Time started, first thing in the morning. All the children were gathered in one room. They were indeed seated in a circle on the floor, but being preschoolers, they were squirreling around, talking and laughing. The teachers were busy calming them down and reminding them to be quiet. Then Mrs. Weeratunga walked into the room. She observed what was happening, calmly walked around the outside of the circle and sat down in her spot. In a voice no louder than a conversation with a friend, she said, "We're going to play the Quiet Game. Let's see how quiet you can be." Within 3 heartbeats, you could have heard a pin drop in that room.

These children knew Mrs. Weeratunga loved them, heard them and respected them. They would do anything she asked. You should have seen how hard they worked to put on the Christmas program and the Spring program every year for their parents. It was so beautiful to see what patience and service and love and respect can create.

Not to do wrong, to do good, and to purify one's
mind, that is the teaching of the awakened ones.

~ Dhammapada, Sayings of the Buddha

RAISING TEENAGERS

Peter was the father of teenagers when I first met him. His wife, Jolie, was away at a chiropractic college in another state and only came home every other weekend. So at that point, Peter was essentially raising the boys by himself (their sister was already in college). Since his sons were friends with a college classmate of mine, their household quickly became our "home away from home" for us college kids.

Peter was fully engaged as a father and a friend, and yet detached at the same time. He never tried to solve your problems; instead he would listen in such a way that you could see them more clearly yourself.

His younger son was a stranger to no one—he'd just walk up and make friends with anyone. This clearly wasn't Peter's own comfort level, but he watched his son and realized that because he was fearless, he tended to ward off any unpleasant experiences. Rather than trying to make his son more like him, he accepted Tom and supported him, even striving to become more like him.

One day, his older son told him, "I want to become even better than you Dad." And then he realized how that sounded and immediately apologized. But Peter couldn't have been prouder. "Of course you must be better than me—that's how the world advances!"

All things are our relatives; what we do to
everything, we do to ourselves.
All is really One.

~ Black Elk

MEETINGS

This last story came to me third or fourth hand, but it still brought tears to my eyes.

The Bahá'í World Center is located in Haifa, Israel. It is home to the Universal House of Justice, an elected body of nine people that governs the affairs of the global Bahá'í community. It is also a World Heritage site with beautiful gardens and buildings housing the work of administering a worldwide community. Many Bahá'í youth from around the world choose to give a year of service there during or after their college years.

A friend of mine went to visit one time and came back with all kinds of stories from the youth. One young man described his first days there. He was on a break one day and an older gentleman stopped by and joined him. He asked the youth where he was from and how he liked being there. The youth answered his questions and then asked the man what he did. He simply said, "I attend a lot of meetings." They talked some more and then the man left.

Immediately the other youth crowded around this young man and asked, "Do you know who that was?! He's a member of the Universal House of Justice!"

The humility of this man still inspires me, a person who shares the responsibility of governing a global community of millions of people... and yet just says "I go to a lot of meetings." To this day, I still don't even know his name.

The sage stays behind, thus he is ahead.
He is detached, thus at one with all.
Through selfless action,
he attains fulfillment.

~ Lao Tzu

PUTTING IT INTO PRACTICE

How do we foster within ourselves and within our group the qualities of:

- Service
- Patience
- Humility
- Detachment
- Purity of Motive
- Radiance of Spirit
- Attraction to the Divine

As with anything we're trying to learn, these things take practice. Here are a couple of ideas to get you started:

1. **Find an example.**
   Look for these qualities around you. Who do you observe who exercises patience? How do they do it? Thank them for it. Describe in detail what you see and the effect it has on the people involved. Who do you observe who does their work in the spirit of service? How does this change the dynamics of your group? Share with that person what effect it has on you.

2. **Catch each other in the act.**
   Perhaps in your group you can make a game of noticing these qualities in each other. In our family, we had a jar and a bunch of flat-bottomed florist's "gems" in cheery colors. Whenever we noticed a family member demonstrating one of these qualities, we put a gem in the jar.

After a while, though, we realized we couldn't remember the acts themselves, so we set up a "good deeds wall" in the breakfast nook. We bought a bunch of calendar cut-out shapes that teachers use on the classroom calendars (leaves for September, pumpkins for October, turkeys for November, etc.). Each time someone demonstrated one of these qualities, we wrote it up on a cut-out shape and put it on the good deeds wall. It just made you feel good to read all these stories in the mornings while eating breakfast.

WHAT DOES THIS MAKE POSSIBLE?

Can you imagine what could happen if everyone is working on developing their own inner qualities? And noticing these qualities in others? What kind of an environment could we create together?

WHAT IS YOUR EXPERIENCE?

- Describe a time when you observed true humility.
- How did that experience affect you?
- When have you observed or experienced:
  - Patience?
  - Detachment?
  - Service?
  - Radiance?

Chapter 5
EXPRESS YOUR VIEW

In order to really understand an issue, we need to be able to look at it from all sides. And since no single person has all the information, we need to hear from everyone.

Each of us has a different way of looking at things. Some of us see vistas. Some of us see details. Some of us look at the practical side of things. Some of us seek deeper spiritual meanings.

All of these views are important and necessary if we are to get to the truth of an issue.

Consultation provides the means to discuss a matter thoroughly. The goal is to do so in such a way that does not create discord or ill-will:

- Each person is completely free to express his or her thoughts and opinions.
- No one belittles the thoughts of another.

- If someone expresses an opposing view, one must not feel hurt.
- Each person listens carefully to all views, whether they agree with them or not.
- It is only when the matter is thoroughly examined and all views are expressed that the truth will be revealed and the right course of action made clear.

They must then proceed with the utmost
devotion, courtesy, dignity, care and
moderation to express their views.

~ 'Abdu'l-Baha

GATHERING ALL THE VIEWS

I was involved with a group that was debating whether to hold its meetings online or in person. Everyone had an opinion and some were strongly felt.

But as we delved deeper into what each person's experience was, we found out that some people have really busy schedules and online meetings save time. Others live far away, so online meetings eliminate a lengthy commute.

On the other hand, for some, the technology really wasn't working, so we didn't actually see their faces. Some found it difficult to freely express their views when they had to stop and unmute their microphone each time they wanted to talk. Some found it difficult to read nonverbal cues in an online setting.

If we were to go deeper still and explore this issue in light of spiritual principles, we would start to ask different questions: How do we assess the value of online meetings in terms of justice, equality and universal participation? How does unity fit in?

The more we listen, the deeper we go, the more there is to share. And the more clearly we begin to see the whole picture.

What would happen if we truly developed the skill of voicing our view clearly and reached for deeper and deeper levels of understanding?

He speaks at the right time, in accordance with
facts, speaks what is useful, speaks about the law
and the discipline; his speech is like a treasure, at
the right moment accompanied by arguments,
moderate and full of sense.

~ Buddha, the Word (The Eightfold Path)

PUTTING IT INTO PRACTICE

Many times I get caught up in the clamor of my own thinking and I want to rush to share my opinion on a subject. Or I hold back, thinking my view is not important, not popular or contradicts what has already been said. I remain silent because I don't want to cause difficulties. But then I realize that each view is important, not because it is *the* truth, but because without all the views, we can't *arrive at* the truth.

Here are some thoughts about expressing one's view.

1. **Share your piece.**
   We each have a piece of the puzzle and if we go to either extreme, it's not helpful:

   If we insist on our own view, we create a blockage. If we withhold our view, we create a hole.

2. **Listen.**
   At first, we tend to just voice our opinions. But as we grow quiet inside and seek stillness, as we listen to what others are saying, we start to see more deeply. This is the place where insight comes from. As we quiet our inner chatter even more, we start to see what is emerging. The deeper we listen, the more richness there is to observe and share.

3. **Go deeper.**
   The whole point of consultation is to arrive at the truth of the matter. There are levels of understanding as we move from the surface to the heart level. We

go from rattling off our opinions, to really thinking about an issue and analyzing it, to connecting deeply around the heart of the matter. In all of this, we each still only see a part of the puzzle. But as we share what we are observing, together we form a more complete picture.

- **Opinion**—This is often where we start. Share your view and listen to the views of others. What do you observe?
- **Experience**—When we talk about our experience with an issue, we start to understand what's behind people's opinions on the matter.
- **Insight**—Often this comes as a sudden flash as you make connections between different aspects of the issue.
- **Understanding**—What have you learned from engaging with the issue? What new awarenesses have emerged for you?

4. **Apply spiritual principles.**
   The tenor of the consultation changes when we start examining an issue at the level of principle.

   - How does **justice** play a role in this issue?
   - What if we look at it with the lens of **equality?**
   - What about **universal participation**? Who is affected by this issue?
   - What if we examine the issue from both a **scientific** *and* a **spiritual** view?
   - How does **unity** relate to this issue?

They are guided unto gentle speech;
they are guided unto the path
of the Glorious One.

~ Qur'an, Sura 22

WHAT DOES THIS MAKE POSSIBLE?

Can you imagine what could happen if we could actually see an issue from all sides? What if we truly welcomed all voices to the table? What if we really understood who is affected by the issue and invited them to join the conversation? Can you imagine how robust our solutions could be?

WHAT IS YOUR EXPERIENCE?

- What has helped you express your view, even when it was difficult?
- When have you been part of a group that moved beyond just voicing opinions to thinking/sharing more deeply about an issue?
- What tools or practices have you found helpful in getting to this deeper level of thinking and sharing?

Chapter 6
LET GO

Consultation is like playing with Legos® or Tinker Toys™. We each come to the table with a collection of bricks (our views and opinions). If we hang on to our bricks, we end up with just a jumbled pile of building blocks. But if we offer those bricks to the group and combine them all, we can actually build something together—a skyscraper, a spaceship, or even an entire city.

The same is true of consultation. If we insist on our own opinions, we just end up tangling with one another. But if we share our views and let go of them, then, as a group, we can sift and sort through all the ideas until we fully understand the matter and see how best to proceed.

They must in every matter search out the
truth and not insist upon their own opinion, for
stubbornness and persistence in one's views will
lead ultimately to discord and wrangling and the
truth will remain hidden.

~ 'Abdu'l-Bahá

LIFTED UP

This is a set of journal entries over the course of a couple days...

Wednesday

Letting go... I certainly have lots of experience of hanging onto my opinion. What helps me let go? Realizing in the first place that I'm hanging on. Recognizing when I get into that rebellious mode. Awareness is a big part of it. And willingness. Trust in the process. Trust that the best course of action will be found. Trust in Divine Power to guide the process.

There's definitely an arrogance involved—I feel like I need to lead this discussion; I know what's right. But the truth is, I can only see so much from my vantage point. There's always more to an issue than I can perceive by myself. In order to see the whole picture, we need the views of everyone involved. It requires a willingness to look beyond my view, a desire to see the whole picture, a letting go of the illusion that I already see the whole picture, a valuing of the contributions of others.

Thursday

Our group is having a meeting tonight and there is one issue we need to discuss that is emotionally charged. I feel anxious about being able to be detached. Oh! That helps! I just pictured the noise and tumult "out there," not in my face. The issue is complex and there are strong reasons for both sides of the argument.

Letting Go... What I'm finding is that I need to not only let go of my own view, but I also need to let go of my anxiety about other people's views. And about the discussion itself. This skill of being fully engaged and yet detached at the same time is quite challenging. Fully engaged—in that you are listening carefully to every view that is expressed, because you never know where the spark of truth will emerge. Fully engaged—in that you fully express your view of the situation, because every perspective is valuable. And detached—in that my view is just one piece of the puzzle. The whole point of consultation is to seek truth. It's not just a clash of opinions.

Friday

Yesterday I had the most extraordinary experience. I met a friend for coffee in the afternoon and we went for a walk. She was telling me about her frustrations with a certain project in the community. It was one of those cases where there was tremendous potential, yet the effort put forth didn't quite measure up.

She asked what my experience was. There was a slight pause and then I just felt this spirit flow through me— like a wind; it lifted me up as if I had wings and carried her right along too. I found myself talking about our little project and yes, it could have been so much bigger. But for our community, it represented a huge shift in thinking. I found myself talking about *what is* and encouraging that—fanning that little flame and helping it grow. What *did* happen was this: People came out of the woodwork. People invited their friends to participate. We found a way to engage the children in quiet creativity next to the adults who were attending the program. We held the event in a public place and made it welcoming for anyone to just walk in and join us. What did happen? We started to catch a glimpse of who we are and what we can accomplish together—we are capable of so much more than we dreamed!

This wasn't a formal consultation, it was just a conversation between two friends, approaching an issue from very different perspectives. But we ended up seeing a wholeness that wasn't visible to either one of us before. I didn't come into it with a goal of convincing her to see things a certain way. In fact, during that pause after she asked the question, I didn't even know what to say. Then this flood of inspiration surged through me, lifting me as it lifted her. It was the most incredible thing! By being willing, in that moment, to be of service to my friend, I found my words and actions guided by a force beyond me. Phew! If that's what letting go looks like, I want more of it! It was so powerful and clarifying and energizing.

That was the afternoon. In the evening, our group had its meeting with that emotionally-charged issue. As I drove over there, I just asked for help. I didn't want to lose that ability to let go and be lifted by that flow of spirit. I didn't want to get tangled in the noise and tumult of the inter-actions. I realized that I did have a definite opinion on the matter. But with that experience of being lifted so fresh in my mind, I also realized that I was willing to let go of my opinion to get to the truth—and that was more important than what I thought was right.

The meeting proceeded. When that issue came up, luckily enough time had passed that the emotions had calmed down. There were a couple of clarifications that were needed, but in the end, it seemed like we all under-stood the complexity of the issue. We came to a decision that everyone agreed on and that actually propelled us forward. No turmoil, no fuss, just a sober recognition that we are all being called upon to reach deeper and do more so that this world can be healed.

When I let go of what I am,
I become what I might be.
When I let go of what I have,
I receive what I need.

~ Tao of Leadership, John Heider

PUTTING IT INTO PRACTICE

It's so easy for me to believe that I'm right and that my view is the correct one, especially if I've put a lot of effort and thought into the matter. I've worked hard to get here!
So how do we let go of our view?

1. **Remember we each just have one piece of the puzzle.**
   No matter how much effort I put in, I'm still just one person. I can only see so much.

   Actually, what I'm finding is that it's a relief to know I don't have to try to see all the different sides of an issue on my own. In school, we are taught to do our own work: we are graded as individuals, we must present a complete treatment of the subject on our own.

   When I actually slow down and listen to others' perspectives, I begin to realize how very little I actually see. It becomes much easier to let go of my own view because I'm intrigued to hear what else will show up.

2. **Seek truth.**
   Another thing that helps me let go of my view is to remember that the point of consultation is to seek out the truth of the matter at hand. When I'm focused on seeking truth, I've got something better to do than defend my position. And when someone offers a perspective that gets closer to the truth, I'm actually free to abandon my position altogether in favor of progress.

3. **Listen.**

    Letting go also becomes easier as I get better at listening. When I listen deeply, both to those around me and to my own heart, the process becomes more like mining for gems of wisdom rather than a debate between varying points of view. There's more joy of discovery and less defensive maneuvering. And it's a whole lot more fun!

4. **Ask how.**

    "How" is a powerful question and can help lift us out of our own opinions and into seeking solutions. "How do we move forward with this?" "How can we gain a deeper understanding of what is really going on here?"

5. **Keep learning.**

    Sometimes we hang onto our views because we don't want to admit that maybe we didn't have a complete understanding of the issue. But this is an essential part of the process. If we insist on our views, we can't progress, we can't move forward—we end up stuck in territory we already know.

WHAT DOES THIS MAKE POSSIBLE?

Can you imagine how much faster our teams can move when no one has to defend their ego? What would it be like to create an environment where everyone feels free to express a view and let go of it completely?

WHAT IS YOUR EXPERIENCE?

- When have you experienced letting go of an opinion or view that was important to you?
- What happened as a result?
- What effect did it have on the group?

Chapter 7

SEEK TRUTH

Consultation is about searching out the truth. Without this goal, we quickly devolve into warring opinions. But truth has gotten a bad rap over the years. Too many times we've seen one person or group try to impose their "truth" on others. This is a distortion.

Truth is one. It's like light. Light may shine in many different lamps, but it is still light. We may view it through different colored lenses, but it is still light.

> Consultation bestoweth greater awareness
> and transmuteth conjecture into certitude.
> It is a shining light which, in a dark world,
> leadeth the way and guideth.
>
> ~ Bahá'u'lláh

Seeking truth is like looking at this lantern. Each of us sees just one side of the lamp. It's important to share what we see: the pattern, shape and color of the facet we are looking at, the glimpses of light that shine through.

But just sharing our views is not enough. We need to search deeper and find the truth, the light—the flame *within* the lantern. That's what we are trying to get at as we describe what we see. By expressing our views *and* seeing beyond them, we can piece together a description of the flame inside.

PARENTING

When my daughter was growing up, she and I would sometimes get into a tussle over some issue or another. I'd try to be "the Mother" and get control of the situation. And, like any healthy, independent human being, my daughter would resist that control.

Round and round we'd go until I finally realized it was up to me. I took a breath and stepped back. Sometimes it took a while, but eventually I'd be able to come back and say, "Look, here's what's going on for me."

As it turned out, more often than not, the root of the conflict was some inner turmoil I was dealing with in my life. Once I got clear on what that was and said it out loud, everything got easier. My daughter was then able to describe what was going on for her and we were able to get to the truth of what was really happening between us.

We ended up with a much deeper appreciation for each other and for the struggles we each were facing. Developing that understanding helped each us of navigate our own trials much better.

It was only when I let go of what I thought should happen and squarely faced what was actually happening for me, that the conflict got resolved.

PUTTING IT INTO PRACTICE

So how do we get to the truth of a matter? What kinds of questions do we need to ask?

1. **Gather the views.**
   Perhaps one of the first questions is… Do we have all the views? Is there anyone missing from the table? Depending on the issue, this could mean any number of things:

   - Who is directly affected?
   - Who is indirectly affected?
   - What do our youth have to say?
   - Have we heard from our elders?
   - What insights do our children have to offer?
   - Have we given everyone a chance to speak— women, men, old, young, introverts, extroverts, thinkers, dreamers… ?

2. **Clarify the issue.**
   Then there are questions about the issue itself:

   - Do we fully understand what the problem is?
   - Do we know why this issue is important?
   - Have we framed it correctly?
   - What if we look at this issue from a broader perspective?
   - Do we see a pattern? What does it tell us?
   - Are we even asking the right questions?

3. **Identify the principles.**

   Once we understand what the issue is, one powerful way to illuminate truth is to think about the issue in terms of spiritual principles or universal values:

   - What role does justice play in this issue?
   - How does this issue relate to equality? To equity?
   - What if we look at this issue through the lens of unity?
   - How do we incorporate diversity?
   - What does science tell us about this issue?
   - What is our moral/ethical responsibility?
   - What would universal participation look like?
   - What are the educational implications of this issue?

These are examples of the kinds of questions that can be helpful in seeking the truth. What others can you identify?

A man should look for what is, and not for
what he thinks should be.

~ Albert Einstein

WHAT DOES THIS MAKE POSSIBLE?

What would happen if all our systems and structures in this world were aimed at seeking truth? What would be the implications for our justice system? Our education system? Our governance system? What could we achieve if we were dedicated to seeking truth?

WHAT IS YOUR EXPERIENCE?

- When have you had to work closely with someone to find an answer together?
- What process did you go through to arrive at your answer?
- Did the answer surprise you? In what way?

Chapter 8
SUPPORT THE DECISION

Have you ever made a decision as a group and then discovered that one or more members were bent on undermining that decision? What happened? Not much gets accomplished, does it? Then bad feelings set in and people start bickering with one another.

This is why the consultation process extends beyond the decision itself to the support necessary to carry it out.

In consultation, once all the views have been shared and fully investigated, the group then comes to a conclusion and decides on a course of action. Ideally the decision is unanimous, but sometimes it must come to a majority vote.

In either case, it is essential for everyone to fully support the decision, *whether they agree with it or not*. If there is dissension and disunity, the truth will not come to light and the path forward will not be clear. But if the group is unified and the decision is wrong, it will quickly become apparent and a new decision can be made.

...even if the decision is wrong, "as it is in unity
the truth will be revealed and the
wrong made right."

~ 'Abdu'l-Bahá

A DECISION CORRECTED

A few years ago, my Dad died suddenly. He lived in a tiny, remote astronomy community in rural Arizona, where the skies are dark and the stars are bright. My brother and sister and I flew in from opposite corners of the country and were immediately faced with a million decisions.

If you've ever had to settle the affairs of a loved one who has passed, you know what I mean: there were funeral arrangements to make, people to inform, family accommodations to arrange, financial and legal affairs to settle, the house to sort through... and all of this while you're dealing with your own emotional state and that of everyone else around you.

Talk about a pressure cooker for testing our consultation skills! Somehow the three of us managed to get through it all. There were definitely rough patches, but, for the most part, we kept talking things through until we came to a consensus. Sometimes it took a long time and sometimes we needed a cool-down period, but we were generally able to come to an agreement on the issues at hand. It certainly helped to focus on what Dad would want; it kept us in that mode of being of service, rather than wrangling for our own opinions.

One decision we made actually turned out to be the wrong one. We'd opted to just hold a small graveside service for the family and then have a community gathering/potluck later. One or two of us may have had some misgivings, but we'd all agreed, so that's what we set out to do.

It turns out we really didn't understand the culture of this tiny community of 150 people. Being so remote (the nearest grocery store is 60 miles away), everyone has to rely on each other. Not all the astronomers live there year-round, so when they leave, neighbors take their remaining garbage to the truck that comes once a week. They organize their own volunteer fire and rescue team and everyone participates in the drills. If someone needs something, neighbors show up to help. They all get together regularly for potlucks, especially during the holidays when both the tavern and the café shut down for the season.

And when someone dies, everyone is affected.

We arrived at the cemetery for what we thought would be a quiet graveside service. To our surprise, the whole town showed up. People kept streaming in from all over.

We'd planned a short program; Bahá'í burials are very simple—there's just one prayer and then the rest is up to the people involved. So we said the Prayer for the Departed and opened it up for people to share whatever was in their hearts.

What they shared were stories—story after story of Dad's kindness, his friendliness, his willingness to help, his quiet habit of driving around just keeping an eye on things, his gentleness, his gentlemanliness, and yes, his standard order for dinner at the tavern. (Dad was a man of simple wants and when he found something he liked, he stuck to it.)

The whole experience was beautiful, touching, tearful, tender and funny. It was a day I will never forget.

We'd made one decision but ended up with something entirely different. For me, it was a powerful reminder of how, when you work in unity, your work is guided and even your missteps are corrected with grace and ease.

Hold fast, all together, to God's rope,
and be not divided among yourselves.

~ Qur'án 3.103~5

PUTTING IT INTO PRACTICE

So how *do* we support the decision? When a decision is right on track, everyone is on board and we all feel great about making it a reality. No problem. Yet, sometimes there's doubt about the decision and that's when things get challenging.

1. **Commit to action.**
    In consultation, everyone gets behind the decision and implements it. This means putting your whole-hearted effort into it. It's not enough to just pay lip-service and then take no action.

2. **Refrain from criticizing the decision.**
    It's really easy to fall into old patterns. After all, we're so used to criticizing everything around us, from the government to our latest encounter with a retail chain. And granted, there's a lot that needs to be improved. But this is one area where criticism won't help.

    If I criticize the decision or drag my feet, I just cause turmoil, making it harder to see what is actually happening. Did the project fail because this actually was a bad decision or because of the turmoil and contention? If we all pull together and implement the decision, we'll quickly see if it was on track or not. And often, like in the case of Dad's funeral, the course-correction can be quite gentle.

WHAT DOES THIS MAKE POSSIBLE?

Can you imagine how quickly our teams can move with whole-hearted support behind their decisions? Can you imagine how nimble our groups can become—adapting to changing landscapes, swiftly learning from mistakes, propelling the work forward? Just think what we can accomplish!

WHAT IS YOUR EXPERIENCE?

- When have you supported a group decision and found confirmation that it was the right decision?
- When have you supported a group decision even when you felt it was wrong? What happened?
- What is your experience with maintaining unity in a group?

Chapter 9
CONCLUSION

Human potential on an individual level is incalculable. Yet one person, alone, can only accomplish so much. Just think what we can do when we come together, seek truth and embark on unified action.

The problems we face as a humanity are entrenched, intertwined and global in nature. No one person or nation can solve these problems alone. It will take all of us—those from the East and those from the West, from the North and from the South. It will take every race, every nation, every religion, every people on earth to solve these problems.

We each have a different perspective and each perspective is vital if we are to dig down to the heart of the matter and develop solutions that benefit everyone. Impossible as this may seem, it is well within our grasp.

We humans are indeed one family. We live on this small planet and our future is in our hands. What happens in one part of the world, really happens to all of us. We urgently need tools that help us work together for the benefit of all people, not just an elite few.

Consultation is such a tool. It is being used at the United Nations, in large international bodies, at national conferences around the world, in regional and local endeavors, in professional organizations and businesses, in schools and in families.

The more we practice these principles of consultation with our work teams, in our families and in our communities, the more skilled we become. We'll be able to bring these skills into all arenas of human endeavor: education, business, governance, environmental stewardship, art, industry and community organizing.

Can you imagine what our world would be like if we humans drew upon our richly diverse human legacy:

- The ecological wisdom of our Native American brothers and sisters.
- The mindfulness wisdom of our Asian brothers and sisters.
- The innovation wisdom of our American and European brothers and sisters.
- The community wisdom of our African brothers and sisters.
- The family wisdom of our South American brothers and sisters.
- The connectedness wisdom of our Oceanic brothers and sisters.

What if we humans could weave all these strengths together? Just think what we could accomplish!

QUICK REFERENCE

For your reference, below is a summary of the ideas outlined in this book:

1. **Consultation:** a process of group decision-making that is built on truth-seeking and strives to find the best solution for all parties involve.

2. **Oneness of humanity:** All people are members of one human family. In consultation, our diversity allows us to see an issue from all sides. Our unity allows us to integrate these perspectives and chart a wise course of action.

3. **Harmony and inspiration:** The more we see each other as champions of truth, the easier it is to weave our strengths together and find solutions.

4. **Inner work:** Consultation takes practice and a focus on developing the inner qualities of patience, humility and a desire to serve.

5. **Express your view:** Each person shares his or her thoughts and opinions and everyone listens carefully to all the views.

6. **Let it go:** Once you've stated your view, it's no longer yours; it belongs to the group.

7. **Seek truth:** The group explores all the views to search out the truth of the issue.

8. **Support the decision:** Once the group comes to a conclusion and decides on a course of action, everyone puts their full support behind the decision.

BONUS CONTENT

Consultation is a powerful tool that can be used in any group. To make it easy to share these ideas with your team, we've created a set of slides and handouts just for you:

- PowerPoint slide show: full-color slides explaining the principles of consultation
- Full-color handout for printing
- Black and white handout for printing

Download your free toolkit at:

ourprosperousworld.com/ConsultationToolkit

ACKNOWLEDGEMENTS

I am grateful for all the people who have helped make this book a reality. Thank you to Beverlee Pattonallen, JoAnn Siebe, Lyn Martin, Martha Wagner and Jami Cannon for your insightful comments.

Thank you to Otto Scharmer and the entire U.Lab team at M.I.T. for helping me focus on how we are learning together. Thank you to Stephanie Fleming for starting me on this journey in the first place.

Thank you to Kristina Golmohammadi for your joyous love of learning and for your stimulating conversations over the years.

A special thank you to Mom, Meg and Martin. You have taught me so much.

Bruce Poinsette, thank you for your expert editing skills.

Carlos Brito, thank you for your beautiful cover design and illustration.

Laura Boyle, thank you for your great interior design.

Finally, my deepest gratitude to Ric and Emily. You are a constant source of inspiration and encouragement to me. I feel honored to walk this journey with you.

ABOUT THE AUTHOR

Sara DeHoff is a freelance writer and learning artist, addressing audiences in such diverse fields as healthcare, high tech, energy efficiency and various nonprofits.

An unwavering believer in the power of the human spirit, she draws on her 30 years of experience in working with groups of various kinds to write about building community, working together and continuous learning.

After completing her B.A. in the radical alternative environment of Evergreen State College, she went to the other extreme and earned her M.Ed. at Harvard. She has lived, worked and studied in China, Japan, Taiwan and the Czech Republic. Sara currently resides with her husband in the hills of rural Oregon.

You can reach her at:
ourprosperousworld.com
sarad@ourprosperousworld.com
Facebook/ourprosperousworld
@HumanProsperity

Made in the USA
Middletown, DE
28 June 2019